science
essentials

The perfect **exam revision** guide

food, blood
and bones

Denise Walker

First published in paperback in 2010 by:
Evans Brothers
2a Portman Mansions
Chiltern Street
London W1U 6NR

Series editor:
Harriet Brown

Editor:
Katie Harker

Design:
Robert Walster
Adam Williams

Illustrations:
Q2A Creative

Printed in China

© Evans Brothers Ltd 2006

British Library Cataloguing in
Publication Data

 Walker, Denise
   Food, blood and bones. - (Science
essentials. Biology)
    1.Nutrition - Juvenile literature
2.Blood - Juvenile
   literature. 3. Bones - Juvenile literature
   I.Title
   572.4

ISBN: 9780237539764

Contents

Introduction

Food is an essential part of our lives. We need to eat regularly to give our bodies energy to carry out life processes. The quantity and the types of food

that we eat are also important – vital nutrients help to keep the body in good working order.

This book takes you on a journey to discover more about the importance of diet for good health. Find out about different types of food, learn how food is absorbed into the body and discover the way in which our bones and muscles work together to keep us on the move. You can also find out about famous scientists, like Claudius Galen and William Harvey. Learn how they used their skills to find out how blood transports vital nutrients around the body.

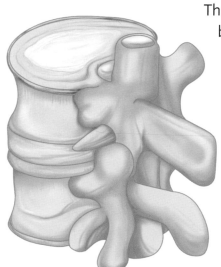

This book also contains feature boxes that will help you to unravel more about the mysteries of diet and health. Test yourself on what you have learnt so far; investigate some of the concepts discussed; find out more key facts; discover some of the scientific findings of the past and see how these might be utilised in the future.

Food is something that many of us take for granted. Now you can understand more about the ways in which a good diet can help to keep us fit and healthy.

DID YOU KNOW?

▶ Watch out for these boxes – they contain surprising and fascinating facts about diet and health.

TEST YOURSELF

▶ Use these boxes to see how much you've learnt. Try to answer the questions without looking at the book, but take a look if you are really stuck.

INVESTIGATE

▶ These boxes contain experiments that you can carry out at home. The equipment you will need is usually cheap and easy to find.

TIME TRAVEL

▶ These boxes describe scientific discoveries from the past, and fascinating developments that pave the way for the advance of science in the future.

ANSWERS

At the end of this book on pages 46 and 47, you will find the answers to questions from the 'Test yourself' and 'Investigate' boxes.

GLOSSARY

Words highlighted in **bold** are described in detail in the glossary on pages 46 and 47.

Eating for life

Food is an essential part of our lives. If you didn't eat or drink your body would be deprived of the energy it needs to grow, maintain and repair itself. Today, the wide variety of foods on display in our supermarkets shows just how many different food types are available. We have a more varied diet than our ancestors, but the quantities in which we eat these foods can affect our health and wellbeing.

YOU ARE WHAT YOU EAT?

Food and fluids are essential to maintain the body's **cells** and to keep fit and well. Your body needs a variety of foods at regular intervals to keep in top condition.

It is important to eat a varied diet because you need to supply your body with all the **nutrients** that it needs. Eating too much (or too little) of one food type can cause **malnutrition**. Malnutrition literally means 'bad feeding' and although this condition is usually associated with underdeveloped parts of the world, malnutrition can affect anyone.

A CLOSER LOOK

What exactly do we mean by a balanced diet? Five basic food groups contain the essential nutrients that the body needs:

▶ Carbohydrates
▶ Proteins
▶ Fats
▶ Vitamins
▶ Minerals

▲ A poor diet has caused this child to become malnourished.

A balanced diet means eating the right proportion of these five food groups (we need to eat more carbohydrates, for example, than vitamins and minerals). Fibre and water are also important parts of a balanced diet. Fibre doesn't provide the body with nutrients but it keeps the digestive system working effectively. Water is one of the most important substances that the body needs. Your cells are mostly made of water and need a constant supply of fluid to work properly. Water also helps to transport materials around the body and to flush out **toxins** that could cause harm.

▲ Eating a variety of foods is the best way to keep healthy.

EATING THE RIGHT STUFF

The following table shows examples of foods that make up a varied diet.

FOOD GROUP	SOURCE
Carbohydrates	Pasta, bread, rice, potatoes
Proteins	Meat, fish, cheese, milk
Fats	Eggs, dairy products, dips and sauces
Vitamins	A – carrots B – egg yolk C – oranges and lemons D – fish oil
Minerals	Iron – liver Calcium – milk Iodine – fish
Fibre	Bran cereals, sweetcorn, celery, tomatoes, cucumber

GETTING THE BALANCE RIGHT

How much food you need to eat depends on your age, your gender and your body size. Larger people need more food because they have more cells to maintain. Men also tend to eat more than women because they have more muscle tissue to sustain (muscles use a lot of energy).

Some governments advise the public about following a healthy diet. In the US and the UK such guidelines include:

▶ Eat at least five portions of fruit and vegetables each day. These can be fresh, frozen, tinned, dried or a glass of juice.

▶ Grill, bake, poach, boil, steam or microwave instead of frying or roasting. Or you could 'dry roast' without adding any fat.

▶ Choose lean meat and trim off the fat and skin.

▶ Eat more starchy foods such as pasta, rice, potatoes, cereals and pulses (beans, peas and lentils). These should make up about a third of your diet.

▶ Try to eat fish at least twice a week. You can eat up to four portions of oily fish a week, such as mackerel, sardines and trout, but avoid having more than this.

▶ Reduce the amount of sugar in your diet.

▶ Don't add salt to your food and be aware of the salt content of ready-prepared foods.

▶ Drink plenty of water each day, especially in hot weather or if you exercise.

▶ It is also important to keep a check on the quantities of food portions in your diet and to take regular physical exercise.

▲ Oily fish, such as sardines, are a good source of proteins, vitamins, minerals and fatty acids that have been found to protect against the risk of heart disease.

TIME TRAVEL: DISCOVERIES OF THE PAST

▶ Scientists have been studying the diets of our early ancestors by looking at fossil remains and analysing ancient hair samples. Their results show that between two and three million years ago, early man also followed a varied diet of fruits, leaves, meat, vegetables and seafood.

Sometimes, eating a balanced diet is not possible due to particular circumstances. Some people follow a special diet for medical or religious reasons. Others choose to follow an alternative diet because of their personal beliefs. In some parts of the world, food is scarce and people have to eat whatever is available.

AVOIDING MEAT

Vegetarians and vegans are now common across the world. Some simply do not like the taste of meat. Others think that animals should not be eaten – perhaps for religious reasons. A vegetarian diet is one where animal meat products are avoided. A vegan diet avoids all products relating to animals, including eggs, cheese and milk. Sometimes, strong vegan principles mean that a person will also avoid animal products that aren't food-related, such as leather bags or shoes.

▲ In Hindu communities, cows are regarded as sacred and beef is not eaten.

Meat provides us with protein, iron (a mineral) and fat, but vegans and vegetarians can eat other things to supplement these food types. Fat can be found in dairy products; protein can be found in dairy products and fish; and iron can be found in green vegetables, such as spinach. Vegans may find it more difficult to follow a balanced diet. They need to eat plenty of legumes (lentils and beans) and nuts to get the protein and fat they need.

◄ Vegetarian dishes are becoming common in western diets because some people choose not to eat meat.

INVESTIGATE

▶ Write a list of all the foods you have consumed in the last 24 hours. Don't forget to include drinks and snacks. Now compare your list to the recommended guidelines. In which areas are you lacking in food types? Do you have too many of some food types?

Although vegetarians and vegans can adapt their diet to include all food groups, there are times when particular care is needed to ensure a healthy lifestyle. For example, during pregnancy a vegetarian or vegan would need to eat more protein to keep themselves and their unborn child healthy.

SLIMMING DIETS

In the western world so many food types are now readily available that many people have difficulty controlling the amount of food that they eat. Eating more food than your body needs can lead to health problems such as **obesity** (see page 15). To curb this problem, special diets have become popular in recent years with people who are trying to lose weight. The 'Atkins diet' for example, is a diet plan composed mainly of fat and protein, with very little carbohydrate. Named after the late Dr Atkins, an American **cardiologist**, the diet claims that eliminating carbohydrates from your diet encourages the body to burn fat and therefore lose weight. Research studies have shown that followers of the diet have lost twice as much weight than those following a low-fat diet. Other weight-reducing diet fashions include a high-fibre eating plan that reduces calorie intake while keeping you feeling full for longer, and the grapefruit diet, which claims that half a grapefruit before every meal provides the body with 'fat-annihilating' **enzymes**.

However, many diets have come under criticism from medical authorities because they are thought to be unhealthy eating regimes. Doctors say that replacing carbohydrates with large quantities of meat, for example, supplies the body with too much fat that can lead to health complications such as high **blood pressure** and heart disease (see page 37).

(see page 15)

(see page 37)

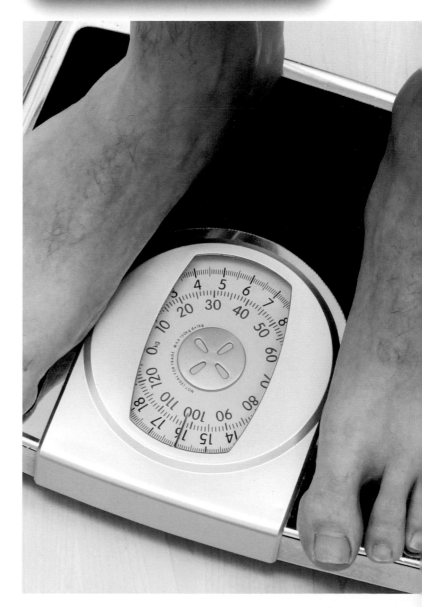

▲ Weight-loss diets have become popular in western society.

Food groups

A balanced diet gives your body the nutrients it needs to carry out important chemical processes. When your body needs more food (or fluid) you will begin to feel hungry (or thirsty). The main food groups provide your cells with the energy they need to carry out vital processes and to keep your body on the move.

CARBOHYDRATES

All living cells release energy when they carry out their daily tasks. This energy comes from a reaction between the food you eat and the oxygen you breathe – a process called **respiration**. We need large quantities of carbohydrates (starch and glucose) in our diet to respire effectively.

Two other types of carbohydrates provide us with energy in a different way. Simple sugars (sometimes called 'refined sugars') provide us with an instant burst of energy that the body uses very quickly. This type of sugar can be found in sweets and chocolate. Simple sugars are a useful energy boost, but they are not the best way to provide a constant supply of energy.

▲ Chocolate provides a burst of energy but tends to make us feel tired a short time later.

Complex carbohydrates are a much better source of energy, capable of nourishing your body over a longer period of time. Complex carbohydrates are found in foods such as pasta and bread.

PROTEINS

Your body needs nutrients from your food to replace worn-out cells and to repair any damage. Proteins are molecules that are made up from smaller parts called amino acids. When protein is consumed it breaks down and then reforms again in human tissue. Proteins also make enzymes – molecules that are needed by all living things to speed up reactions in the body (see page 20). Proteins are found in foods such as meat, fish, cheese and milk.

◄ Pasta contains complex carbohydrates which are a good source of slow-burning energy.

VITAMINS AND MINERALS

Your body needs small amounts of vitamins and minerals to work properly. Minerals are simple chemicals found in most foods. Examples include iron (which helps red blood cells carry oxygen around the body) and calcium (which helps to build strong teeth and bones). Vitamins are more complicated chemicals. A diet lacking in vitamins can cause a range of deficiency diseases.

FATS

Fats are important in our diet because they provide us with energy. Instead of dissolving in our blood like other foods, fats accumulate around tissues and cells so they can be used to maintain cell membranes. Stored fat under the skin is also a good source of insulation.

TEST YOURSELF

▶ Design a table showing the main food groups, their use in the body and problems that an excess or deficiency may cause.

There are two types of fat: saturated fats from animal foods, and unsaturated fats from plant foods. Eating fat in moderation is an important part of a balanced diet. However, unsaturated fats are generally healthier – too many saturated fats can lead to health problems linked to blood circulation and the heart (see page 37).

▶ A lack of vitamin D has caused this boy to develop rickets – a disease that causes the bones to soften and bend as the body grows.

▼ The uses of common vitamins and minerals.

VITAMIN OR MINERAL	EXAMPLE SOURCE	USE	DEFICIENCY
Vitamin A	Carrots, liver	Good vision and healthy skin	Bad night vision and unhealthy skin
Vitamin B1	Yeast, beans, egg yolk	Healthy nerves and growth	Beri-beri*
Vitamin C	Oranges, lemons	Tissue repair and resistance to disease	Scurvy
Vitamin D	Sunlight, fish oil	Strong teeth and bones	Rickets**
Iron (mineral)	Liver, cocoa	Healthy red blood cells	Anaemia
Calcium (mineral)	Milk, green vegetables	Strong teeth and bones	Soft bones
Iodine (mineral)	Fish	Thyroid gland	Goitre***

* Beri-beri is a condition that can damage the heart and nervous system. Symptoms include pain, tingling or loss of sensation in hands and feet, muscle wasting and increased heart rate.
** Rickets is a condition resulting in soft bones that cannot support the weight of a growing body. Symptoms include bone pain, slowed growth in children and increased risk of fractures.
*** Goitre is a condition in which the thyroid gland becomes swollen (a gland situated across the front of the neck, just below the voice box). Symptoms include swallowing and breathing problems.

WATER

Every day your body loses about two litres of water as you breathe, sweat and go to the toilet. Because your cells mostly contain water, fluid makes up about two-thirds of your body. It is important to replace the water that you lose by drinking liquids and eating foods that contain water. Although we can survive for up to 60 days without solid food, we cannot survive for more than a few days without water. In extreme circumstances (in the aftermath of an earthquake, for example) some people can survive for several days if they have access to water. Health guidelines suggest that we should drink about two litres of water a day to replace the fluids that we have lost. We should also drink more in hotter weather or when we exercise.

FIBRE

Fibre is a substance found mainly in plant matter. Fibre forms an important part of our diet even though we are unable to digest and use it in our bodies. Fibre aids the movement of undigested foods through the body. Without fibre we would not be able to pass faeces comfortably and would quickly become constipated. Research has shown that fibre also contributes towards our general health. Fibre reduces the risk of bowel diseases and has been found to reduce the amount of **cholesterol** in our blood, a fatty material that is caused by eating saturated fats (see page 37). Fibre also makes us feel full for longer which is good for those trying to lose weight. Vegetables, fruit and wholemeal bread are rich in fibre.

◀ Water is one of the most important substances that your body needs.

DID YOU KNOW?

▶ Babies have an area of brown fat around their necks. Very young babies are not able to shiver to keep themselves warm so this brown fat is used when it gets cold. It helps the body to generate heat and maintain a healthy temperature.

▶ Americans used to use the term 'limey' to describe sailors from the UK because they were often seen sucking limes when they came off their ships. This was because the sailors were trying to combat the effects of scurvy – a disease often caused on a long voyage when fresh fruit and vegetables are in short supply. Symptoms of scurvy include joint pain, bruising, receding gums and general weakness.

▶ Scientists have found that what you eat can affect your mood – some nutrients have a direct affect on the brain. Proteins, such as meat, are thought to help you to feel more alert, while carbohydrates are thought to be good for relaxation. Researchers also believe that 'comfort food', which is generally high in fat, helps to suppress stress hormones, making you feel more cheerful. Too much of these foods however, can lead to excessive weight gain.

Energy requirements

Thanks to the energy that we get from carbohydrates and fats we are able to go about our daily lives. But sometimes it can be difficult to get the balance right. If we eat too little we may feel faint and tired; if we eat too much we are in danger of becoming overweight.

MEASURING ENERGY

Next time you go shopping, take a look at the labels on packaged food. You will see that as well as detailing the ingredients and food types that a product contains, the label also indicates the amount of energy that the food provides. Energy from food is described in units called kilojoules (kJ) or kilocalories (kCal). Joules and **calories** are small amounts of energy so we use this larger unit where 1 kJ = 1,000 joules and 1 kCal = 1,000 calories. Nowadays, kilojoules are more commonly used (1 kJ = 0.24 kCal).

Your body uses different amounts of energy when you are active and when you are at rest. When you sleep your body uses about 4 kJ a minute to keep your lungs working, your heart beating and your brain functioning. Walking uses about 20 kJ per minute, running about 40 kJ per minute and more vigorous exercise about 80 kJ per minute.

▶ Food labels outline the amount of energy a product contains as well as the ingredients.

WHAT FOOD TYPES DO WE NEED?

We mainly need to eat carbohydrates to aid the process of respiration (see page 10). When carbohydrates are in short supply, the body burns fats for energy. This explains the basis of many weight-reducing diets (see page 9). If both carbohydrates and fats are in short supply, the body begins to burn proteins for energy. When these proteins are parts of the body itself we say that a person is 'starving'. In underdeveloped parts of the world, where crop failures or war can lead to famine, starvation is a major form of malnutrition with serious side effects.

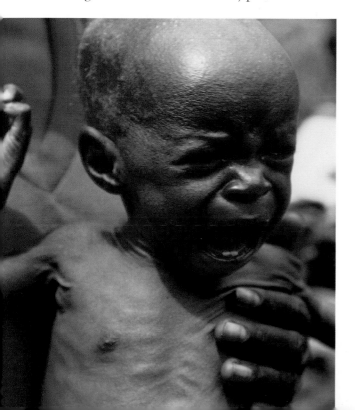

◀ This starving child is at risk of symptoms such as poor bone formation, blindness and damage to the immune system.

HOW MUCH ENERGY DO WE NEED?

We all need different amounts of food to keep ourselves healthy. A gram of carbohydrate provides about 17 kJ of energy; a gram of fat about 38 kJ; and a gram of protein about 20 kJ. Most of our energy requirements in a balanced diet should come from carbohydrates.

The amount of energy that you need depends on three factors:

▶ The energy that you need to perform basic functions, such as breathing and maintaining body temperature. This is called the **basal metabolic rate** (BMR). It is on average about 7,000 kJ per day.

▶ The amount of exercise or activity that you do. A physical activity, such as running, can raise the BMR rate to 12,000 kJ a day.

▶ The amount of food that you eat – eating uses up energy during the digestive process.

When these three factors are put together it is possible to calculate an average daily energy requirement. Remember that these are only average recommendations – everyone is different.

AVERAGE DAILY ENERGY REQUIREMENTS

	Male	Female
8-year-old	8,500 kJ/day	8,500 kJ/day
Teenager	12,500 kJ/day	9,500 kJ/day
Office worker	11,000 kJ/day	9,800 kJ/day
Physical worker	15,000 kJ/day	12,500 kJ/day
Pregnant woman		10,000 kJ/day

As we get older, our energy requirements increase to a maximum in adulthood. This is because our basal metabolic rate needs more energy to support growth and development, and we need more energy to digest the larger food portions that we eat. If you are physically active you will need more energy to fuel your movements. Pregnant women also require a little more energy to feed their growing child. In later life we need less energy. This is because elderly people tend to be less active and their muscles become slightly smaller.

▲ You need to eat more if you are physically active.

OBESITY

With so many food types readily available in the western world, overeating has become a serious problem. Weight gain is also increasing because we are exercising less – transport and 'arm-chair' entertainment have become a way of life and snacks are available at every turn. Our lives are a far cry from those of our ancestors, who had to hunt for their food!

If you eat more than your body needs over a significant period of time, this extra energy is converted into fat and stored in tissues around the body. When the level of fatty deposits increases to a certain limit, a person is described as obese. Body fat is measured using a scale called body mass index (BMI) that divides your weight by your height. The BMI scale considers a person's weight and height so that different body shapes can be taken into account. Even so, a scale of this kind cannot be accurate in every case. For example, athletes with large muscles will have a larger BMI because muscle weighs more than fat.

HOW 'BIG' IS THE PROBLEM?

The problem of obesity is spreading. More than 72 million US citizens (about thirty-four per cent) are now obese and there are about 300 million obese people worldwide. Although the US and Europe are most commonly affected, newly developing nations such as China are quickly catching up. A significant proportion of the world's population are now risking their health through overeating.

HEALTH RISKS

Obesity can cause a whole range of health issues. If fat accumulates in blood vessels, the heart has to work harder to pump blood around the body and this may lead to heart failure (see page 37).

Obesity has also been linked to diabetes, a disease in which the body does not have enough insulin (a **hormone**) to control sugar levels in the body. Symptoms include frequent urination, excessive thirst, unusual weight loss and blurred vision. The disease can sometimes be fatal. Scientists have found that if a person accumulates excess fat and sugar in their bloodstream, the body's cells can become resistant to insulin. With so much extra fuel around, the cells begin to ignore signals to take more sugar from the blood. Over time, the body's cells may become permanently resistant to the effect of insulin.

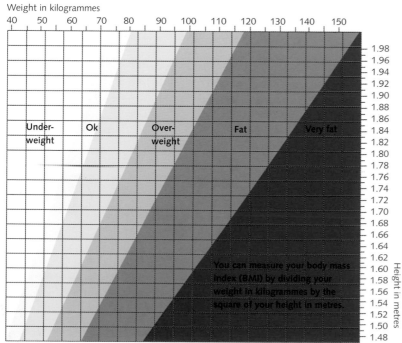

Weight in kilogrammes

You can measure your body mass index (BMI) by dividing your weight in kilogrammes by the square of your height in metres.

◄ This type of graph is commonly used by doctors to indicate weight levels. A body mass index (BMI) of 20-25 is a healthy weight; a BMI greater than 25 is an indication of excess weight; and a value over 30 is considered to be obese.

CAUSES

Obesity occurs because people consume food containing more energy than they are able to use up. Modern lifestyles are a contributing factor – in the past, children played outside instead of watching television or playing computer games. Western populations also use extensive transport systems to get around. If physical activity is limited, the amount of energy that we 'burn off' is reduced. Fast food outlets that supply instant meals when you're on the go have also become a way of life for many people. These meals are usually high in saturated fats. Social class is thought to play a role in obesity, too. High fat foods are often cheaper than healthier alternatives – a tempting option for poorer families.

Sometimes, **genetics** plays a role in obesity. Studies are beginning to identify specific genes linked to obesity, although it is still not clear why some people can maintain a balance between the food they eat and the energy they use. Understanding more about the genetic causes of obesity may help to find new options for prevention and treatment. A tendency to store fat is believed to be the result of thousands of years of evolution in an environment where food sources were scarce. People who could store energy were more likely to survive periods of famine and to pass this gene onto their offspring.

▶ A combination of diet and exercise is the best way for people to lose weight.

DID YOU KNOW?

▶ Babies born in the USA in 2000 have a 32 per cent chance (male) and a 38 per cent chance (female) of developing diabetes in their lifetime. This risk has been rising in the USA and similar trends have been seen in Europe. Changes in western diet are blamed.

SOLUTIONS

Although obesity may be a genetic condition in some cases, the disease can still be managed with lifestyle changes. A combination of diet and exercise is the most common method of losing weight. In more extreme cases, however, radical surgical procedures such as gastric bypass surgery are used – a procedure that closes off most of the stomach so that patients can no longer eat large quantities of food. Any kind of surgery brings risks but gastric bypass surgery is a popular option for many people who are desperate to lose weight.

Governments are becoming more aware of the obesity 'epidemic' engulfing the western world. Food labelling is now becoming a common requirement and public health campaigns are encouraging healthier lifestyle options.

ANOREXIA

Although obesity is fast becoming the latest epidemic of the modern western world, another equally serious (but quite different) weight problem is suffered by a small group of people. This condition is an eating disorder called **anorexia nervosa** (or 'anorexia' for short).

According to ideal weight guides, a BMI of less than 20 is considered to be underweight. However, a BMI of less than 16 is much more serious and indicates that a person is suffering from anorexia. People with anorexia diet intensely in search of an unrealistic body mass and shape. The condition is most common in women between the ages of 15 and 25, but men can also be affected. In western cultures, advertisements on television and in magazines often portray a slim figure as the 'norm'. Young women may see thin models as a role model and take weight loss to the extreme.

People with anorexia can lose weight in many different ways. Dieting, excessive exercise, vomiting and sometimes the use of **laxatives** ensure that the body quickly uses up any food that has been eaten. Anorexia is largely a psychological disorder and sufferers may be very secretive about their condition. Psychological therapy may be needed to encourage a patient to eat more (or in some cases, force-feeding may be necessary if the condition has become serious).

◄ Slim models in western society encourage young girls to aspire to an unrealistic body shape.

DANGERS

Extreme weight loss can cause a number of health risks. Muscles grow smaller if the body begins to burn muscle tissue for energy (see page 13). This in turn causes tiredness and a general feeling of exhaustion. If your **immune system** becomes weak you are less likely to fight infections. Excessive weight loss can also interrupt a woman's menstrual cycle and may affect fertility. The body's chemical balance can also change, leading to deficiency diseases, heart failure and possibly death.

BULIMIA

Bulimia is an eating disorder that is related to anorexia. Instead of starving their body, bulimics eat large quantities of food in a short time (known as 'bingeing') and try to prevent any weight gain by dieting, vomiting, exercising or using laxatives.

DID YOU KNOW?

▶ Anorexia is common in particular sports where body image is important – such as dancing, gymnastics and ice-skating. In 1994, Christy Henrich, a world-class American gymnast died from anorexia. Christy began intense dieting after being told that she needed to lose weight by a competition judge. She resorted to anorexia and bulimia as a way to control her weight and the eating disorder eventually took her life. When Christy died, at the age of 22, she weighed less than 20 kilogrammes.

The digestive system

Once you have eaten your food, the process of digestion breaks it down into smaller parts so that your body can absorb the goodness that it contains. Digestion is both a mechanical and a chemical process. The body uses special chemicals to break food down into more manageable parts. Physical processes like chewing or mixing food also help to disintegrate the food that we eat. A number of different body parts are used in this complicated process.

Digestion begins in the mouth where, as you chew your food, your lips, teeth, tongue and saliva help to turn large, dry pieces of food into small, soft lumps that can be easily swallowed. Saliva contains an enzyme called 'amylase' that encourages the chemical breakdown of food. Amylase works mainly on carbohydrates. Your tongue is also covered in taste buds to help you to enjoy your food and to taste when food has gone bad.

Muscle relaxed

Muscle contracted

Food

Muscle contracted

Food

Muscle relaxed

Oesophagus

OESOPHAGUS

When food has been chewed it enters the oesophagus (food pipe). The muscular walls of the oesophagus push your food along in a process called **peristalsis** – rather like squeezing toothpaste out of a tube. The action of swallowing also triggers the epiglottis (a piece of cartilage hanging at the back of the throat) to close over the trachea (wind pipe). This prevents food from going down the wrong way and causing you to choke.

STOMACH

The stomach can hold up to 1.5 litres of food and drink. Some of the food is dissolved by stomach acid and the stomach muscles help to mix food and enzymes together (an action called churning). A small ring of muscle around the top of the stomach opens to allow food to pass through and prevents stomach acid from reaching other body tissues where it could cause damage. The stomach also contains two other chemicals: a thick substance, called mucus, prevents stomach acid from damaging the stomach lining; and an enzyme, called pepsin, begins the digestion of proteins.

◄ Your mouth is the first part of the digestive process.

THE SMALL INTESTINE

Once your food has churned in the stomach for a couple of hours, it passes into the duodenum (the first part of the small intestine). Bacteria in the intestines help to break down your food and produce certain enzymes to speed up the process. Two important liquids are also added – pancreas juice and bile. Pancreas juice is made and secreted by the pancreas and contains enzymes that break down carbohydrates, proteins and fats. Bile is a yellowish liquid made in the liver and stored by the gall bladder. It contains chemicals that neutralise the harmful stomach acid, enabling enzymes to work. Bile also helps to break down large pieces of fat so the enzymes can work more effectively. Your food then enters the jejunum and ileum where your digested food passes through the intestine lining so that your blood can carry the goodness to wherever it is needed in the body (see page 24).

Over 400 different types of bacteria live in your digestive system to keep it healthy. These 'good' and 'bad' bacteria usually live in harmony but if the balance changes you can become unwell with sickness or diarrhoea. Antibiotics are used to treat bacterial infections of the stomach. However, they also kill the good bacteria, too. Eating foods that are full of good bacteria (like yoghurt and cottage cheese) can help to retain a healthy balance.

THE LARGE INTESTINE

The small intestine leads into the large intestine through the caecum and into the colon. By this time most of the nutrients from your food have been absorbed. The remaining fibre, dead cells, bacteria and water are pushed along the colon by peristalsis and, as water is absorbed, the undigested food forms a solid waste called faeces. This waste is stored in the rectum and passes out of the body through the anus when you visit the toilet.

PARTS OF THE DIGESTIVE SYSTEM

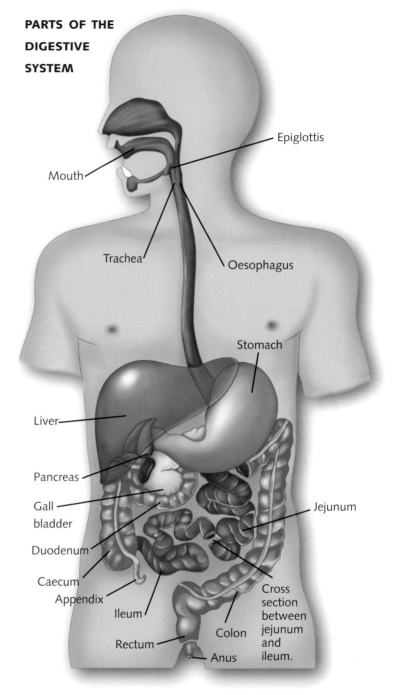

Epiglottis
Mouth
Trachea
Oesophagus
Stomach
Liver
Pancreas
Gall bladder
Duodenum
Caecum
Appendix
Ileum
Rectum
Colon
Anus
Jejunum
Cross section between jejunum and ileum.

DID YOU KNOW?

▶ The acid in your stomach is strong enough to burn rocks!
▶ Thanks to the process of peristalsis, astronauts can still swallow their food when they are upside down.
▶ The tubes of your digestive system would measure about nine metres if they were uncoiled and stretched out.

Enzymes

Chemical and physical changes are happening all the time in your body. It's these processes that help your cells to build new tissues, convert your food into energy and dispose of waste materials. The reactions that take place are speeded up thanks to special chemicals called 'enzymes'. Enzymes are essential for digesting food but they are also used in other body processes, such as stimulating the brain and repairing cells, tissues and organs.

WHAT ARE ENZYMES?

Enzymes are proteins found in our cells that speed up cellular reactions. They are essential to living creatures because without them, chemical reactions within our cells would occur too slowly to sustain life. Respiration and digestion are two processes that rely heavily on the action of enzymes. Enzymes help to break our food into the size and kinds of substances that our body can absorb and then help our body to release energy from this food. We need this energy to keep on the move and for our cells to carry out vital processes. If any one of the 2,000 enzymes in our body fails to work properly it can cause a serious illness.

PROPERTIES OF ENZYMES

Enzymes behave in different ways but they have five main properties in common:

1) Enzymes are reactive

Enzymes are described as working like a 'lock and key' – with the enzyme as the lock and the substrate (the substance it is working on) as the key. For an enzyme to work on a substrate, the two must fit together. They join at what is called the 'active site'. However, because the fit is slightly imperfect, the enzyme puts the substrate under strain. This encourages a reaction that speeds up the chemical process.

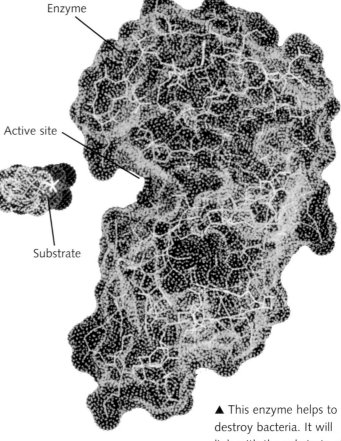

Enzyme

Active site

Substrate

▲ This enzyme helps to destroy bacteria. It will link with the substrate at the active site.

2) Enzymes are specific

Enzymes come in different shapes and sizes. Most enzymes will only react with a small group of chemical compounds while others will only work with one particular substrate with which they have a very close fit – just like Cinderella and her slipper.

3) Enzymes do not appear to be used up

When the substrate and enzyme lock together, a reaction occurs which changes the substrate into a different substance called the product. The product breaks away from the enzyme and the enzyme can be used over and over again.

4) Enzymes act at certain temperatures

Enzymes and substrates move around faster as they get warmer which increases their activity. However, above 40 °C, the specific shape of an enzyme is destroyed beyond repair and the substrate can no longer fit into the active site. The enzyme changes (becomes '**denatured**'), like boiling an egg, and this change cannot be reversed.

5) Enzymes act in certain acidity levels

Some enzymes like acidic conditions, such as the acid levels in your stomach, whilst others prefer neutral conditions. If an enzyme is subjected to a level of acidity that it doesn't like, it will not work effectively (or work at all).

▶ In an enzyme reaction the substrate changes into a different substance (the product).

Enzyme　　Substrate　　Product

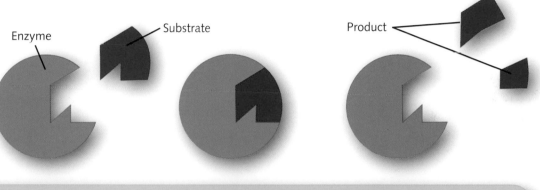

Did you know?

▶ During a fever our body temperature can rise from 37°C up to 40°C. This can be very dangerous because our enzymes can become denatured (changed permanently) and no longer function. If we are cooled again, and not too many enzymes have been denatured, we can survive on those that are still functioning before our body replaces the enzymes we have lost.

▶ Some microscopic organisms, called 'extremophiles', can survive in extreme environments, such as acid hot springs or the scorching temperatures of volcano vents. These organisms can survive in acidic conditions, or when temperatures exceed 100°C, because their enzymes have adapted to suit such extreme environments. The discovery of extremophiles has greatly expanded the areas of Earth now considered to be habitable for life.

Although enzymes have very specific properties, their uses are widespread. Enzymes are essential for chemical reactions within our cells. They are particularly prominent in the digestive system, but also carry out processes like stimulating our brain, relaxing and contracting our muscles and eliminating carbon dioxide from our lungs. Enzymes also have a wide variety of uses in industry. As long as enzymes are used at the temperature and acidic levels that suit them, the results will not be disappointing.

MEDICAL DRESSINGS

One of the fastest acting enzymes in our body is called 'catalase'. This enzyme speeds up the breakdown of hydrogen peroxide, a chemical produced naturally by our cells. Catalase quickly changes hydrogen peroxide into oxygen and water, because in its natural state, hydrogen peroxide can damage or even destroy our cells. Because catalase works so quickly, we are not even aware that our bodies have produced hydrogen peroxide. The medical industry has used our knowledge of catalase to improve the effectiveness of medical dressings. Introducing hydrogen peroxide into the pad of a medical dressing encourages catalase from the wound to react with the hydrogen peroxide, producing oxygen. Oxygen speeds up the healing process and prevents harmful bacteria (that do not like oxygen) from entering the wound.

CLINICAL TESTING STICKS

Clinical testing sticks are used to test for the presence of biological molecules in our urine. This saves the expense of more complicated blood tests and can give a more direct result. Clinical testing sticks are used to test for diabetes and pregnancy, amongst other things. Enzymes contained within the tips of these testing sticks pick up specific molecules through the lock and key mechanism. The testing stick changes colour if a biological molecule is present and the enzymes are activated.

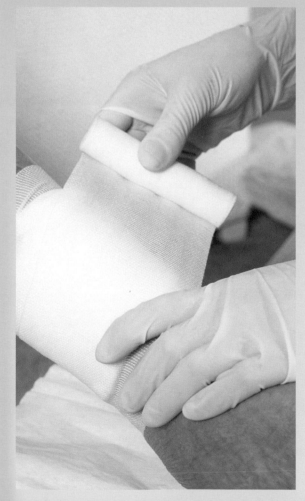

▲ Natural enzymes work with some medical dressings.

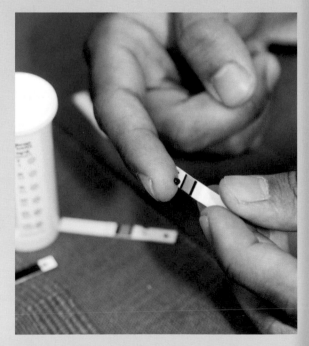

▲ Diabetics test their blood glucose levels regularly.

▲ Enzymes help to get your clothes really clean.

BIOLOGICAL WASHING POWDERS

Many everyday stains on our clothes – like sweat, blood and food – contain protein molecules. Biological washing powders contain enzymes called proteases, which break down proteins and help to remove these stains. To avoid protease enzymes becoming denatured, biological washing powders need to be effective at low temperatures. However, detergent manufacturers are now looking at the enzymes found in extremophiles that are well adapted to high temperatures. If these enzymes can be extracted and studied, in the future we may be able to make our own enzymes that work at higher temperatures.

THE TEXTILE INDUSTRY

Leather is a material taken from the hide of cattle. Untreated leather is a hard material and difficult to wear. Manufacturers make leather softer by adding protease enzymes that remove proteins in the material.

THE FOOD INDUSTRY

Enzymes have a number of roles in the food industry, including the manufacturing of bread, cheese and alcohol. Enzymes can also improve the consistency of the food that we eat.

UNUSUAL USES OF ENZYMES IN THE FOOD INDUSTRY

Use	Purpose
Meat preparation	Enzymes tenderise the meat to make it more tasty
Slimming products	Enzymes convert sugar into a sweeter product that is less fattening
Chocolate	Enzymes are added to liquid chocolate to allow it to flow more easily before it sets
Fruit juice	Enzymes are added to make the juice look less cloudy
Ice cream	Enzymes are added to make ice cream smooth because it has a tendency to be lumpy

6

Absorbing food

Digestion is of no use unless our food can be absorbed into the body. The small intestine is specially designed to absorb the food that has been digested. Here, carbohydrates, proteins and fats are processed and distributed to the parts of the body where they are needed most. Some nutrients are used as building blocks to grow and repair the cells. Others are converted to energy so that the body can move and maintain a healthy temperature.

HOW DOES ABSORPTION OCCUR?

The small intestine is lined with thousands of tiny folds, called villi. Each villus contains a network of blood vessels that absorb the nutrients from runny, digested food. The tiny villi are only one millimetre long, but together they form a surface that is 20 times the area of the skin! This means that as many nutrients can be absorbed as possible. The villi are only one cell thick so food passes through them easily. Villi also have a blood vessel that transfers the food directly to the blood to be transported around the body. Fats cannot be absorbed into the blood, but villi have a 'lacteal vessel' that transports fat to the **lymphatic system**.

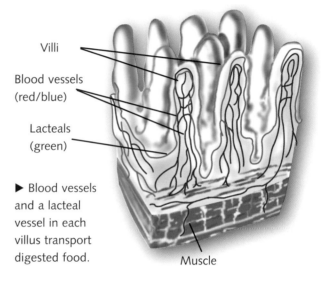

Villi

Blood vessels
(red/blue)

Lacteals
(green)

▶ Blood vessels and a lacteal vessel in each villus transport digested food.

Muscle

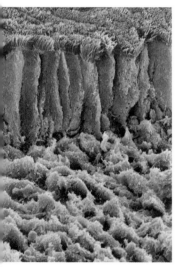

▲ This coloured electron scan shows the villi (orange) and micro-villi (red) that line the small intestine. Magnification approximately x 100.

THE DRIVING FORCES

When your food is squeezed along the ileum, pressure pushes it into the villi. Some digested food is absorbed through the process of **diffusion** (where varying pressure on the surface of a cell encourages substances to move into and out of the cell).

WHAT IS ABSORBED?

Digested carbohydrates and proteins are taken into the blood where they are transported directly to the liver for sorting. The liver helps to filter, store and prepare these nutrients. If too many carbohydrates are consumed, the excess is turned to fat and deposited around the body. Proteins from food can also be changed into specific proteins that the body needs. Proteins from the liver are transported to make new tissues to heal a wound, for example. Excess proteins are excreted via the kidneys.

DID YOU KNOW?

▶ Alcohol can be absorbed directly through the stomach wall. People can feel drunk quite quickly because alcohol bypasses most of the digestive system.

GETTING RID OF WASTE

The human body is designed to get rid of waste products that might be harmful to us. Some obvious examples include the action of coughing and sneezing as well as sweating and breathing out carbon dioxide. When it comes to the digestive system, the body has a series of specialised organs that help to filter and expel waste materials. Undigested food in the large intestine forms a solid waste called faeces. This waste is stored in the rectum. The faeces then pass out of the body through the anus.

WATER CONTROL

The main purpose of the large intestine is to absorb the water from food so the body does not become **dehydrated**. If you are ill with diarrhoea, this absorption is less effective and the body loses a lot of water in the faeces. This can be dangerous if left untreated because the body starts to 'dry up' and cells can't function properly. If you put your hands on your hips, your thumbs will be pointing to the approximate position of your kidneys, near your back (see below).

Water from undigested food passes into the blood where it is taken to the kidneys through the renal artery. Inside each kidney, there are thousands of small tubes called nephrons. As the blood travels near the nephrons, it is under high pressure as it passes from the wide renal artery to narrower blood capillaries – just like a crowd of people walking down a wide corridor and then trying to pass though a narrow door. This high pressure filters your blood because many substances are squeezed out, including important salts, a waste product called 'urea' and excess water. The nephrons are surrounded by blood vessels and as the waste substances pass through them, the kidneys reabsorbs some of the salts and water, passing them straight back into the blood via the renal vein.

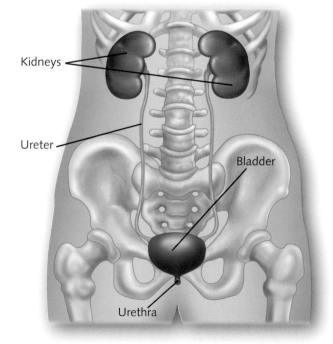

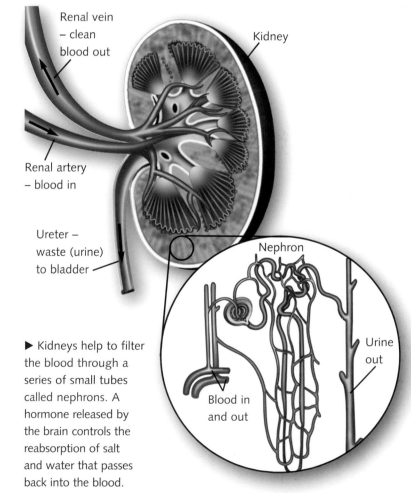

▶ Kidneys help to filter the blood through a series of small tubes called nephrons. A hormone released by the brain controls the reabsorption of salt and water that passes back into the blood.

PASSING FLUIDS

The fluid that remains in the nephron passes to the ureter and then to the bladder. This is the urine that you pass at regular intervals when you go to the toilet. If you drink a lot of water your urine will be pale and dilute because this water has not been reabsorbed back into the blood. However, if you are dehydrated your urine will be darker in colour because it is more concentrated.

HOW MUCH WATER SHOULD WE DRINK?

Your body is two-thirds water and this level must be maintained to keep you healthy. Many parts of the body contain water, including the brain, blood and lean muscle. Every day you lose about two litres of water as you sweat, breathe and go to the toilet. You replace this water by drinking liquids and eating food.

If you are thirsty it is your body's way of telling you that it needs more water. You lose more water in hot weather and when you exercise so it is particularly important to replace fluids at these times. If you become dehydrated, you may feel thirsty and also suffer from headaches. Dehydration is not just a lack of water, but also of important salts such as sodium and potassium that are essential for the healthy functioning of the nerve cells.

▲ It is important to drink more water when you exercise.

DID YOU KNOW?

▶ Athletes who consume large quantities of water during exercise can risk consuming too much water. If this happens, the blood increases in volume and important salts become diluted. If salts are also lost through sweating a low blood salt level may result. This can lead to a lack of functioning of the brain, heart and muscle tissues. This condition is called hyponatremia and early symptoms include fatigue, apathy and nausea. Hyponatremia is often confused with dehydration, but drinking more water can be fatal. Recreational drugs, like ecstasy, have also been known to cause hyponatremia. Ecstasy users can feel thirsty and drink more water than their body needs. They are advised to sip water rather than drink it in large amounts.

Some people find that their kidneys do not function properly because they have been damaged or affected by disease. Although you can survive with just one kidney, if both kidneys fail to function, urgent treatment is needed. Excess water, salts and urea need to be removed from the body to prevent damage to cells that may eventually lead to death.

KIDNEY DIALYSIS

In the short term, people with failing kidneys can be treated using a kidney dialysis machine. This takes the role of a kidney by filtering the blood and removing waste products, before returning the blood back to the patient. A dialysis machine needs to be used for approximately five hours, two or three times a week. Sometimes patients have a kidney dialysis machine in their home; but many need to visit a hospital for treatment. This can have a huge impact on the patient's quality of life as regular treatments are needed. Kidney dialysis patients must be careful to avoid salty foods, such as crisps and crackers, which would otherwise alter the balance of water and salt in their blood and cause further illness.

KIDNEY TRANSPLANTS

Replacing a diseased kidney with a donated kidney can be a cure for many people with kidney failure. However, many patients have to wait a long time before a suitable donor becomes available. Kidney transplants can also be complicated because:

▶ A donated kidney must be a good match in terms of tissue type. A patient's immune system can often react to and reject a new kidney.

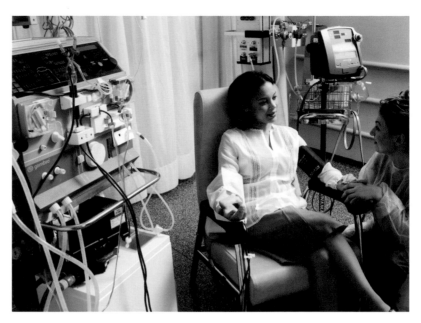

▲ A kidney dialysis machine is used to filter the blood of patients who have kidney failure.

▶ Sometimes, relatives of the patient donate a kidney because they offer the best tissue match. However, this is not always the case.

▶ Some kidney donations come from patients who are being kept alive on a life support machine but who have no chance of recovering from their illness or injuries. It can be difficult for relatives to decide whether their loved ones should have important organs removed for transplantation surgery. In the UK, many people carry donor cards, or have registered online, to say that in the event of their sudden death, they would like their organs to be donated for others to use.

Patients who have had transplantation surgery are given medication to suppress their immune systems as a precaution. Unfortunately this means that they may contract an infection and become ill. Patients need to be kept in sterile conditions for some time after the operation until their immune system becomes stronger, but some kidney transplants still fail nevertheless.

▶ New treatments are being developed all the time that, in the future, may improve the lives of patients whose kidneys have become damaged or diseased.

XENOTRANSPLANTATION

Xenotransplantation is the transplantation of organs across species. The technique had some degree of success when it was first used in 1984 to give a newborn baby a baboon heart – the baby lived for about 20 days. In the future, pigs may be used for xenotransplantation because they have organs that are similar in size to human organs and pigs reproduce quickly. It may also be possible to produce cloned pigs that have genetically-altered organs that are suitable for human use. However, more recent studies have shown that xenotransplantation may not be as safe as previously thought. Some animal organs have been found to transfer viruses that could be harmful to humans.

STEM CELL RESEARCH

Stem cells are cells that have not developed into a specialised cell type. They are found in early **embryos** (although scientists have also recently found them in adult bone and skin tissues). Every cell in your body 'stems' (originates) from this type of cell. Scientists have been looking at how stem cells can be used to restore tissues that have been damaged by injury or disease. Transplanting stem cells into damaged kidneys, for example, might encourage the stem cells to specialise and grow new, healthy kidney tissue. However, although it is quite straightforward to grow kidney tissue, the kidney itself is made up of different cells and tissue types that form a particular structure. To grow a new organ from stem cells would be very difficult. The long-term side effects of stem cell transplantation are also as yet unknown.

TISSUE ENGINEERING

Tissue engineering is a technique developed by two American doctors, Joseph Vacanti and Bob Langer, in 1987. Instead of using stem cells, the technique uses tissue taken from a body that has been donated to medical science. The tissue is grown on specially shaped 'scaffolding' so that it adopts the shape that is required (for example, an ear). To date, scientists have been able to use this technique to grow skin for burn victims. However, in the future it may become possible to grow more complicated tissues like cardiac muscle, muscle tissue and even organs such as kidneys.

▶ Dr Joseph Vacanti and his colleague Bob Langer pioneered the development of tissue engineering.

OTHER DIGESTIVE PROBLEMS

▶ Irritable bowel syndrome (IBS) is a disease in which the large intestine fails to work properly. Symptoms include cramping, diarrhoea and constipation. Some people with IBS find that certain foods (such as alcohol and dairy products) trigger their symptoms. There is currently no cure for the condition but medication and diet can alleviate symptoms.

▶ Crohn's disease is a condition that usually affects the small and large intestines. Symptoms include diarrhoea, pain, weight loss and fatigue. The cause is unknown and there is, as yet, no cure. Treatments try to relieve symptoms. Sometimes, part of the intestine needs to be removed to control the condition.

▶ A number of diseases can affect the liver causing tiredness, weight loss, sickness and diarrhoea. However, because the cells of the liver are able to regenerate themselves, a diseased liver can sometimes return to normal function. Drinking too much alcohol can cause a liver disease called cirrhosis. This is a serious condition because the effects are sometimes irreversible.

Moving things around

7

Some small animals are able to rely on the process of diffusion to move nutrients and waste products between their cells. However, larger creatures, like humans, need a more complicated system (called the 'circulatory system') to transport food, oxygen and vital nutrients around the body. The circulatory system is the body's lifeline and is composed of the blood, blood vessels and heart.

CIRCULATORY SYSTEM

The circulatory system carries nutrients to our cells and removes waste material. The system is also used to regulate body temperature and other levels, such as the amount of sugar and water circulating around the body, to keep it healthy. The heart is the driving force behind the movement of blood, which travels through blood vessels called arteries, capillaries and veins.

THE HEART

The heart lies between the lungs, at the front of the chest, and slightly to the left. Arteries carry blood away from the heart to all of the major organs of the body. Veins carry blood from the organs back to the heart. The heart is made of two pumps that power a separate blood cycle.

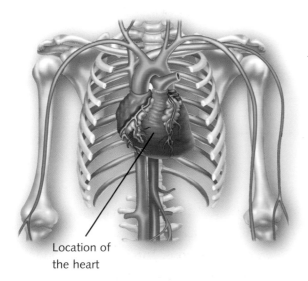

Location of the heart

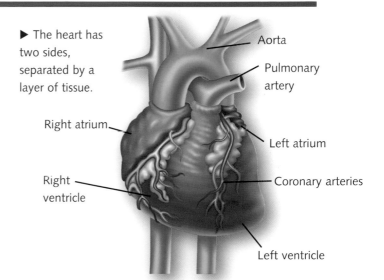

▶ The heart has two sides, separated by a layer of tissue.

Aorta

Pulmonary artery

Right atrium

Left atrium

Coronary arteries

Right ventricle

Left ventricle

The right side pumps blood to the lungs to collect oxygen and back again. The left side pumps **oxygenated** blood to the rest of the body. Once this is done, **deoxygenated** blood returns to the heart and the cycle begins again. Blood passes through the heart twice for each complete circuit of the body which takes about a minute.

ACTION OF THE HEART

When the heart beats, both sides beat together but they are completely separated by a layer of tissue. The blood contained in the two sides cannot mix together, which makes our circulatory system work more efficiently. Some babies are born with a 'hole in the heart' – a hole in the tissue separating the two sides which blood can pass through. This makes the heartbeat less efficient, so doctors try to repair the hole using simple surgery.

The heart has four chambers. The chambers on the top are called atria and those on the bottom are called ventricles. Blood fills up both sides of the heart from the atria, through to the ventricles. When the ventricles are full, valves between the upper and lower chambers close, the heart beats and blood is expelled under high pressure through the appropriate arteries. It is important for the valves to close so that the blood does not pass back out through the atria when the heart beats. The heartbeat is caused by an electrical impulse that the cardiac muscle of the heart generates on its own.

LEAVING THE HEART

Arteries carry oxygenated blood away from the heart (the only exception is the pulmonary artery, which carries deoxygenated blood from the heart to the lungs). When the heart beats, it does so with an enormous force to ensure that all the blood is expelled and delivered to places as far away as the toes. The blood in the arteries is under very high pressure so the artery walls are very thick and muscular. The artery will expand slightly and then

contract as the blood passes through. This also helps to push the blood along. As arteries carry blood at a high pressure, we would bleed to death very quickly if we cut an artery. This is why arteries are located deep within our skin and are difficult to see. Sometimes, arteries must pass over other structures, such as bones in the wrist or tubes in the neck. When this happens it is possible for us to feel the heartbeat as a pulse. The average adult pulse is 70 beats per minute.

▲ You can feel your heartbeat as a pulse in your wrist.

ENTERING TISSUES

Arteries lead into capillaries, which are very thin vessels found in the tissues of our organs. It is here that oxygen and nutrients pass into our body cells (to be replaced by waste products). Capillaries are found in capillary 'beds' that feed a group of cells. Capillaries are very thin which makes it easy for substances to move into and out of them. When blood cells flows into the capillaries they are moving under high pressure and are therefore squeezed out through the capillary bed. This has the effect of pushing oxygen and nutrients into the cells, reducing the level of blood pressure. These substances also pass into our cells by the process of diffusion (see page 24). The blood leaving the capillary bed now contains waste materials.

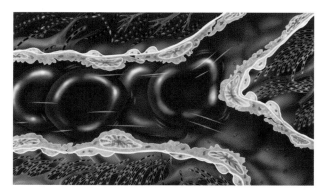

▲ Illustrated red blood cells flowing through a capillary at high pressure. Magnification approximately x 5,000.

GOING BACK TO THE HEART

The blood is at a low pressure when it enters the veins which are situated near the top of our skin and are usually located in muscle tissue. When we expand or contract our muscles as we move about, the blood is squeezed upwards and eventually

INVESTIGATE

▶ Using your two forefingers, feel for the pulse in your neck. Count how many times your heart beats in ten seconds and calculate what this would be in one minute. How does it compare to the average of 70 beats per minute?

DID YOU KNOW?

▶ Very fit athletes have low pulses as a result of their training. The lowest recorded pulses come from Olympic cyclists who can have pulses as low as 20 beats per minute.

▶ The blood flowing through the arteries to the rest of the body is bright red in colour because it is rich in oxygen. Blood returning to the heart in veins is purplish-red because it is lower in oxygen. Arteries and veins often run side by side, with the veins on the outside, where they show blue through the skin. If we cut ourselves, the bleeding from our veins appears red because the blood is exposed to oxygen in the air, which oxygenates it.

▶ Sitting for a long time in one position can sometimes prevent the blood from effectively returning to the heart. If you travel long distances – in an aeroplane, for example – you are advised to stretch your legs occasionally to help your veins to do their work. If the blood becomes static, clots can form in the legs. This is known as deep vein thrombosis (DVT). If a blood clot travels to the heart or the lungs it can be fatal. Those most at risk are the elderly, pregnant women and those who are overweight.

makes its way back to the heart. The blood is now at a lower pressure and generally travelling against gravity. However, veins contain valves, which prevent your blood from flowing backwards. These valves are situated at regular intervals and as the blood flows upwards they close, catching any blood that might fall down.

VEIN VALVES

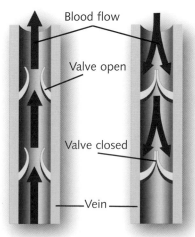

Blood flow

Valve open

Valve closed

Vein

BLOOD COMPONENTS

The blood is made up of billions of cells, all floating in a watery liquid called plasma. Adults have about five litres of blood in their bodies. Children have about half this amount, but grow more blood cells as they get older.

The liquid part of blood is called plasma. Plasma is mostly made up of water, but there are many other substances dissolved within it. These include sugars and vitamins, urea, hormones and **antibodies** that help our immune system.

The 'red' part of blood is made up from three different types of blood cell – red blood cells, white blood cells and platelets. A tiny drop of blood the size of a pinhead contains 5 million red blood cells, 15,000 white blood cells and 250,000 platelets. Each cell type has a different role to play in the working of the body. Blood cells don't last forever. When they die they are broken down by the liver and expelled from the body as waste products. Red blood cells live for about four months and platelets for just one or two weeks. White blood cells may last for just half a day or longer than a year, depending on the type.

RED BLOOD CELLS

Red blood cells look like little doughnuts. They are responsible for carrying oxygen from the lungs, and energy-rich sugars, vitamins and nutrients from food, to the cells around the body. Red blood cells contain a substance called haemoglobin. Oxygen attaches itself to the haemoglobin so that it can be transported around the body. Haemoglobin also transports a substance called nitric oxide that helps with the control of blood pressure, for example by making blood vessels wider when you exercise to transport more oxygen to your cells.

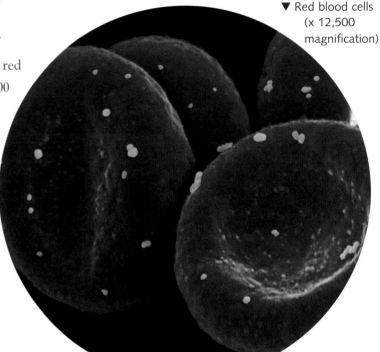

▼ Red blood cells (x 12,500 magnification)

TIME TRAVEL: INTO THE FUTURE

▶ Casualties of serious accidents often need blood transfusions to replace the blood that they have lost. If blood is not replaced quickly, organs can become deprived of oxygen and damaged. Ambulance crews don't carry blood to the scene of an accident – blood types need to be carefully matched to an individual and samples can be wasted because they don't last very long. Instead, ambulance crews carry a saline solution that boosts the amount of fluid in a patient's blood as a temporary measure until they reach hospital. In America, doctors have just started using a synthetic compound that can act as artificial blood in the place of saline. The product, made by a company in Illinois, is called PolyHeme and contains haemoglobin extracted from human blood. PolyHeme can carry oxygen for seriously injured casualties until a blood transfusion can be given. This artificial blood can help to save time, and ultimately save lives.

WHITE BLOOD CELLS

White blood cells have a white appearance. They help to fight infection and are an important part of the immune system. White blood cells engulf harmful bacteria and viruses and disable or destroy them. There are two types of white blood cells that help to fight disease – phagocytes and lymphocytes.

▲ Lymphocyte
(x 7,000 magnification)

▲ This phagocyte is engulfing a foreign body. (x 9,000 magnification)

Phagocytes fight disease by engulfing foreign bodies that appear in the blood. Phagocytes have a lobed nucleus that helps the cell to grow around a foreign body and engulf it. Once engulfed, the cells release an enzyme, which essentially digests the foreign body.

Lymphocytes have a large round nucleus that produces substances called antibodies. Antibodies have a complicated role, but help to fight bacteria in the body. Lymphocytes collect in the lymph nodes when we have an infection and this causes the lymph nodes to swell. Sometimes, when you are unwell you can feel this swelling in your neck.

PLATELETS

Platelets are fragments of cells that help with the clotting process. When we cut ourselves, platelets that are exposed to the air trigger a series of chemical reactions that result in a blood clot being formed. Clotting blood helps to heal cuts on the skin or damage inside the body.

We now know that blood circulates around the body through a network of arteries, veins and capillaries. But at one time, scientists were at a loss as to how the blood travelled and how it transported oxygen and nutrients around the body. Thanks to the work of two prominent doctors – Galen and Harvey, working 1,500 years apart – the mystery began to be unravelled.

GALEN'S THEORY

Claudius Galen was a Greek doctor living during Roman times (129-216 BCE). Anatomy was difficult to study at this time because the Church objected to human dissection (and the Church's influence was very strong). However, Galen

▲ Claudius Galen

expanded his knowledge of the human body by dissecting animals and comparing his findings.

Galen believed that there were two types of blood: venous blood (which we now called deoxygenated blood) and arterial blood (which we now call oxygenated blood). He thought that these two types of blood had different roles relating to the three main parts of the body: the liver, the heart and the brain.

For Galen, venous blood came from the liver and provided nourishment and growth, while arterial blood came from the heart to provide vitality to other body parts. Today, we know that blood is recirculated around the body, but Galen thought that venous and arterial blood were used up. He also believed that the heart sucked blood in as it filled up (rather than acting as a pump as we now know) and that blood pushed itself through the blood vessels unaided.

Galen's theory that there were two distinct types of blood failed to explain properly how the arterial blood came to contain oxygen. Galen believed that arterial blood seeped through hidden holes in the tissue separating the two sides of the heart where it mixed with venous blood. Instead of blood passing through the lungs to pick up oxygen (as we now know) Galen thought that the blood 'mingled' with air in the lungs and a special vessel called the pulmonary vein contained air that mixed with blood in the heart.

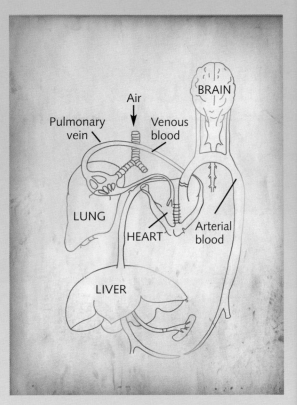

▲ A diagram showing Galen's view of the way in which blood circulates around the body.

Galen's theory, although far from perfect, was generally well received for nearly 1,500 years. Until the 1600s, no alternative explanation of blood circulation was given.

WILLIAM HARVEY'S THEORY

William Harvey was a British physician who lived during the 1600s. Harvey studied at Cambridge University as well as at Padua in Italy where his experiences put him at the forefront of medicine. Although Galen's theories were still strong at that time, Harvey began to look much more closely at the blood system by dissecting animals (most famously the King's deer because Harvey was a royal doctor). Harvey's studies confirmed that the heart worked as a muscle – the ventricles contracted to expel blood and the arteries pulsated because of the shockwave from the beating of the heart.

Harvey initially published his ideas by pointing out the flaws in Galen's theory. He looked for air in the pulmonary vein, but found only blood there. He then discovered that the heart is the centre of a circulatory system. By studying frogs, Harvey showed that the amount of blood that left the heart in a minute could not conceivably be absorbed by the body and continually replaced by blood made in the liver. In fact, Harvey noticed that the amount of blood forced out of the heart in an hour far exceeded the volume of blood in the frog. This showed that the blood must constantly move in a circuit, otherwise the arteries and body would explode under the pressure.

▲ William Harvey

Harvey failed to display the complete circuit through which the blood flows but he came very close to understanding the circular movement of the blood. Harvey couldn't see the tiny connections that linked the capillaries to the veins, but he used a simple experiment to reveal that these connections must exist. First, Harvey tied some material tightly around the forearm so that no arterial blood could flow. The veins in the lower arm were normal but soon became swollen. When the tie was loosened slightly the arterial blood flowed down, but the venous blood could not flow back again. This showed that when the materal was tight, blood had poured down the arteries and then back up the arm within the veins. Harvey's experiment showed that there was an undiscovered pathway in which blood travelled from the arteries to the veins. This new understanding had very little effect on the practice of medicine in Harvey's lifetime, but was to become the foundation for modern research into the heart and circulatory system.

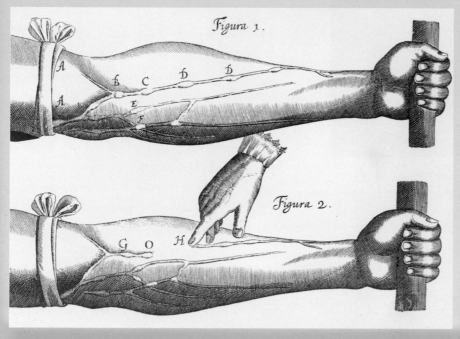

◄ This illustration shows one of the experiments that William Harvey published in 1628. Here, Harvey shows that blood from the arteries is linked to the veins and that the veins flow only towards the heart. When the material on the forearm is tight (figure 1), the veins fill and become swollen. When the material is loosened (figure 2), the veins become less visible as the blood flows again.

Nowadays, people live much longer than they used to. At one time the average lifespan was 40 years, but many people now live to more than twice this age thanks to improved healthcare and more favourable environmental conditions. However, as we grow older, some circulatory diseases become more common.

HYPERTENSION (HIGH BLOOD PRESSURE)

The strength at which the heart pumps blood around the body is called blood pressure. Blood pressure should be kept within a healthy range. If your blood pressure gets too low, you can feel faint because less blood (with oxygen) reaches the brain. High blood pressure is a condition that generally affects older people as the muscular walls of the arteries become less supple and the smaller blood vessels get narrower.

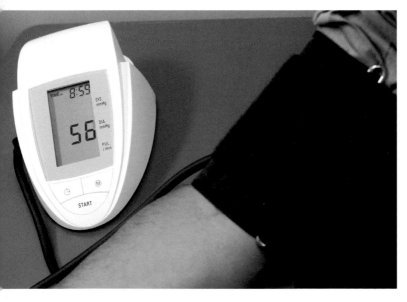

▲ Doctors measure your blood pressure by putting a blood pressure cuff around your arm, inflating the cuff and listening for the flow of blood.

Constant high blood pressure can put unnecessary strain on the heart and cause it to work hard. People with high blood pressure are more likely to suffer a heart attack or a stroke (where a blood vessel in the brain bursts or get

blocked, starving surrounding cells of oxygen). Stroke patients may lose some functioning of their brains and may need to relearn basic tasks such as speaking and walking.

High blood pressure can also be caused by:
▶ Stress
▶ Being overweight
▶ Smoking and drinking
▶ Lack of exercise
▶ Poor diet (including too much salt)
▶ Genetic factors

People with high blood pressure are advised to change their lifestyle to keep their blood pressure at a safer level. Some people are given medication to bring their blood pressure down. Cutting down on fatty food, not smoking and exercising regularly all help to lower the risk.

You may have felt your heart rate increasing when you are scared. Fear or excitement causes the adrenal glands above the kidneys to release a hormone called adrenalin into the blood. This chemical speeds up the heart rate to provide the muscles with extra energy and oxygen, in case you need to fight or run away. If you live a healthy lifestyle this increase in heart rate and blood pressure is not dangerous because your heart is used to coping with sudden changes of heart rate.

ARTERIOSCLEROSIS

Arteriosclerosis is also a disease of the circulatory system. If we eat lots of fatty foods, our blood vessels can become clogged with fatty deposits. This can restrict the flow of blood to important organs of the body, which become deprived of the oxygen they need to work properly.

The cardiac muscle of the heart has many arteries serving it to make sure it receives an adequate supply of oxygen. A painful condition called angina occurs when a narrowed artery restricts the flow of blood to the heart. If a narrowed artery is completely blocked by a blood clot, a painful seizure called a heart attack can occur. A heart attack means that part or all of the heart muscle stops working and can be fatal if not treated promptly, because other organs are soon deprived of vital oxygen.

Arteriosclerosis and heart attacks can be caused by:
▶ A high-fat diet
▶ Obesity
▶ Lack of exercise
▶ Smoking
▶ Genetic factors

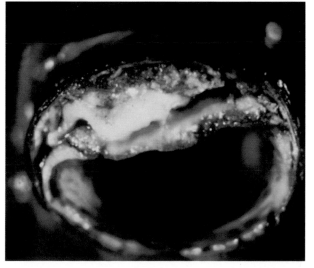

▲ Blood cannot flow well through this narrowed artery.

THE BENEFITS OF EXERCISE AND A GOOD DIET

A low-fat diet prevents fatty deposits from building up in the blood vessels. Saturated fats are the worst culprits because they can be deposited quickly. These fats come from animals (such as those found in meat and dairy products) and are commonly used in processed food. Saturated fats cause the body to make more cholesterol and other fats that don't dissolve in the blood.

Exercise is good for the circulatory system. It helps to burn excess calories that would otherwise cause weight gain. When you exercise your muscles need more oxygen, energy and nutrients than when you are at rest. Exercise temporarily increases the heart rate and blood pressure and the arteries widen to allow blood to flow more freely. This improves the circulation and ensures that the blood vessels are working well.

▲ Exercising regularly is a good way to keep a healthy heart.

Exercising for at least 15 minutes, three times a week, will keep your heart in good condition. Your resting blood pressure will fall and a healthy heart is able to cope with a little extra strain if needed. Studies also show that exercise gives us a sense of wellbeing – if we are more relaxed we are less likely to put unnecessary strain on our hearts.

8

Holding it all together

Our bodies are a system of working organs that keep us healthy and alive. But without a skeleton, you would be a soggy heap on the ground! Your skeleton protects your organs, supports the tissues of your body and allows you to move.

THE FRAMEWORK

When a skeleton is found inside the body it is called an 'endoskeleton'. Some animals, such as crabs and shellfish, have their skeleton on the outside (an 'exoskeleton'). This is useful for protecting the soft parts of their body but can make movement restricted.

▲ This crab has its shell on the outside.

The human skeleton is made up of over 200 bones that link together to form a structure that is light, strong and flexible. Over half of the bones are found in the wrists, hands, feet and ankles. Living bones aren't dry and brittle (like the bones you see in museums) but are tough and flexible and they grow as we get older. The bones are supplied with blood vessels, and nerves that sense pain.

The skeleton has the following functions:
▶ **Support** – humans are able to stand upright due to the strength of their skeletons. The bones that hold us together support the shape we adopt.
▶ **Protection** – vital organs and tissues are protected from damage by the bones of the skeleton. For example, the ribs protect the heart and lungs and the skull protects the brain.

▶ **Movement** – our skeletons are designed to offer flexibility that enables us to move. We have joints that allow bones to move independently of each other. Bones attach to muscles that pull on our bones, making us move.

▶ **Storage** – bones are an important storage for calcium and other minerals.

▶ **Manufacture of blood cells** – the **bone marrow** inside our bones constantly manufactures new red blood cells.

▲ Your skeleton has joints that enable you to move and to use your limbs to carry out different skills.

The skeleton is made up of three main parts:

▶ **Axis** – the central column, which includes the skull, spine and ribcage. The spine (or backbone) is actually a series of 33 very small bones called the vertebrae. These small bones give us the flexibility that we need to move about each day.

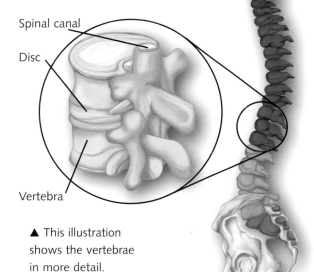

▲ This illustration shows the vertebrae in more detail.

Spinal canal
Disc
Vertebra

The ribcage is important for protecting all of the soft organs found beneath it. This includes the heart and lungs. Organs that are not protected by the skeleton (such as the kidneys) are more susceptible to damage.

▶ **Appendages** – these include all the limb bones. The arms and legs follow the same basic pattern – both have larger bones connecting them to the main frame of the body. Beneath the elbow joint there are two bones in the arm (the ulna and radius) enabling a twisting of the lower arm. In the leg there are also two lower bones – the tibia and fibula. The long bones in the arms and legs are wider at the ends than in the middle, which makes them light and strong.

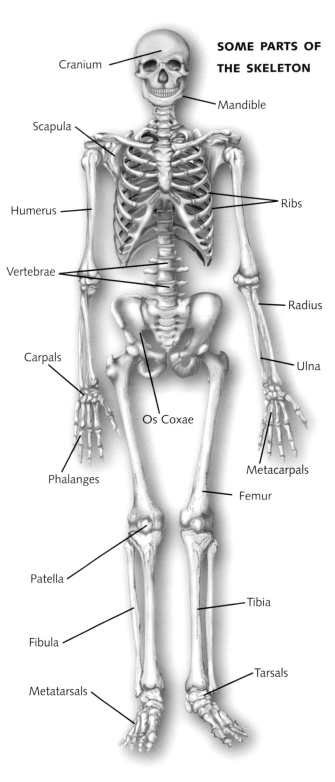

SOME PARTS OF THE SKELETON

Cranium
Mandible
Scapula
Humerus
Ribs
Vertebrae
Radius
Ulna
Carpals
Os Coxae
Phalanges
Metacarpals
Femur
Patella
Tibia
Fibula
Tarsals
Metatarsals

▶ **Girdles** – the girdles connect the bones of the appendages to the bones of the axis. They are the bones of the pelvis and the bones of the shoulders, including the collarbone and shoulder blades.

WHERE BONES MEET

Where two bones meet we have what is called a 'joint'. Joints allow our bones to move freely. There are a number of different types of joints:

▶ Hinge joints

Hinge joints are found in the fingers, knees and elbows. They allow movement in one direction only, like the hinges of a door. Pieces of tissue, called **ligaments**, hold the bones in a fixed position that only allow them to move in one direction.

▶ Ball and socket joints

Ball and socket joints are found in the hips and shoulders and allow us to move these parts in all directions. The end of one bone forms a ball that fits tightly into the end of the other bone (called the socket). The bones are also held together with ligaments, but much more movement is permitted.

▶ The elbow is a hinge joint.

Other types of joint include pivot joints (e.g. the neck), fixed joints (e.g. the skull and pelvis) and gliding joints (e.g. the vertebrae).

◀ The hip is a ball and socket joint formed by the head of the femur and a cavity in the hip bone.

WEAR AND TEAR

Within the skeleton is a rubbery, gristly substance, called **cartilage**, which holds some bones together. Cartilage is also found in parts of the body where more flexibility is needed (such as the elbows and the knees). Cartilage helps to reduce wear and tear when these bones rub together. Some parts of the body, such as the nose and outer ear, are also made from cartilage.

Bones that constantly move and rub against each other would quickly become worn if the joints were not well designed. Hinge and ball and socket joints are also called 'synovial joints'. They are sealed units and contain a fluid (synovial fluid) that reduces friction as the two bones move. The ends of the bones are also covered in cartilage that acts as a shock absorber during movement. Synovial joints are mainly in your limbs where movement is important.

MUSCLE POWER

Although our skeletons are the frameworks on which our bodies are built, we could not move around without muscles. Muscles give the body strength, help us to move around and keep our heart and other body parts moving.

There are approximately 350 muscles in the human body which make up about two-fifths of our body weight. Muscles are found from the face and limbs to inner organs such as the heart, stomach and lungs. You can control the movement of most of your muscles (called skeletal muscles), but others (called smooth muscles) work automatically inside the body.

Skeletal muscles are attached to two bones and as they work, they cause bones to move towards or away from each other. When you bend your knees, for example, muscles attached to the bones above and below the knee do all the work. Muscles also help you to perform smaller movements, such as blinking or raising an eyebrow. Your brain sends a signal to your skeletal muscles when you want to move.

DID YOU KNOW?

▶ Smiling uses about 20 facial muscles, while frowning uses over 40.
▶ Two dentists recently found an unidentified muscle in the skull when they began dissecting the skull from a different angle to traditional dissection methods. The muscle is on average four centimetres long and stretches from the eye to the lower jaw.

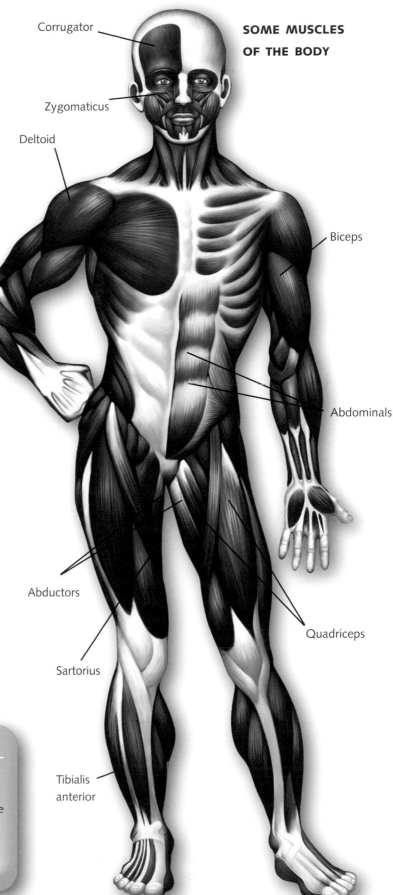

SOME MUSCLES
OF THE BODY

Corrugator

Zygomaticus

Deltoid

Biceps

Abdominals

Abductors

Quadriceps

Sartorius

Tibialis
anterior

HOW DO MUSCLES WORK?

Muscles are able to relax and contract because they are made of fibres that slide over each other. These fibres are bound together in a series of bundles. The end of the bundle is called a **tendon** and tendons are the parts of the muscle that attach themselves to the bones. Tendons should not be confused with ligaments (which hold bones together at joints so they do not drift apart).

When muscles contract, they shorten and the bones to which they are attached are forced to move. Muscles can pull on bones but they can't push against them. Instead, they act in pairs, one on each side of a bone. The muscle pair works as a team – one muscle pulls the bone one way and then relaxes, while the other muscle pulls it back again. For example, when we raise our arm, the biceps muscle contracts and the triceps muscle relaxes. When we lower our arm again, the reverse is true.

▲ Muscle fibres are about the thickness of a hair.

▼ Flexed arm

▶ Extended arm

Biceps Triceps

Biceps Triceps

INVESTIGATE

▶ Look at a piece of raw steak and try to see the groups of fibres. Separate out these fibres by putting the piece of steak into some salt solution. If you have a microscope, examine the pieces under the lens. What can you see?

▶ Ask a friend to hold a ruler up in the air and then release the ruler for you to catch it. Make a note of the reading on the ruler where you catch it. Repeat five times and switch places with your friend. Who has the fastest reaction time?

DIFFERENT MUSCLES

There are three main types of muscles.

▶ **Voluntary muscles** – these skeletal muscles are attached to the bones so you can move them whenever you want to (when you lift your arm, for example). Voluntary muscles can contract and relax quickly, but they soon become tired.

▶ **Involuntary muscles** – these smooth muscles contract and relax automatically in the body. You cannot control the action of these muscles but they carry out some very vital processes. For example, the muscles of the intestines contract and relax to push our food along. Involuntary muscles contract and relax slowly so they do not become tired, like skeletal muscles. Other involuntary muscles include the lining of the hair follicles, the lining of the blood vessels, the stomach muscles that churn our food and the muscles that move urine from the kidneys to the bladder.

▶ **Cardiac muscle** – this is a special type of muscle found only in the heart. It contracts and relaxes about seventy times per minute. The cardiac muscle is an involuntary muscle that works automatically.

REFLEXES

In times of danger we can move very fast – we have sharp senses and our voluntary muscles are quick to respond. Sometimes however, we can act without thinking. This is called a reflex. If we touch something hot, we often move our hand before our brain recognises the pain. Similarly, we can move to catch a falling object before we have even thought to catch it! Reflexes help us to act very quickly, particularly if we are in danger. They are useful in many sports, too.

▲ Having good reflexes is useful when playing ball sports, such as basketball.

Like all body parts, bones and muscles can become damaged or diseased. This can cause problems with mobility and strength. Thanks to advances in medical science however, many common problems can now be treated effectively.

A PROBLEM WITH MUSCLES

Muscular dystrophy is an inherited disease which mainly affects boys. The disease causes the muscles to become weak and wasted. Symptoms usually start when a child begins walking – the child may start to walk at a later age than is usual or they may find that they frequently fall over. The symptoms don't become fully obvious until about the age of three, however, when the child will have difficulty climbing stairs and getting up from the floor. Children with muscular dystrophy also tend to have large calf muscles and wasted muscles at the tops of their arms and legs. Although the condition is largely untreatable, physiotherapists work with muscular dystrophy patients to keep them mobile as long as possible.

A PROBLEM WITH JOINTS

Arthritis is a disorder that causes the joints to become swollen, painful, stiff and eventually deformed. Arthritis is brought on by a swelling of synovial joints and tends to affect the hands, ankles, hips and knees. Persistent swelling can damage the ends of the bones in the joint and the cartilage that covers and protects them. Arthritis is more common in older women.

There is no cure for arthritis. However, the condition can be treated with medication to reduce the swelling of the joints and to slow down any long-term damage. In some cases, where joints have been damaged beyond repair, a joint replacement may be offered.

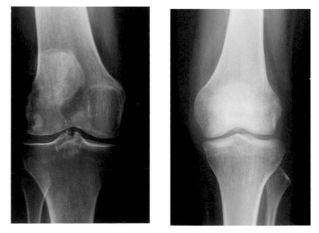

▲ This arthritic knee (left) is more inflamed than the healthy knee joint (right).

◄ This day centre is caring for children with muscular dystrophy.

JOINT REPLACEMENTS

Hip replacement surgery is becoming more and more common as the world's population ages. The hip joint is commonly replaced because a damaged hip has a significant effect on free and flexible movement and therefore quality of life. Hip replacements are made from metal, ceramic or plastic and are designed to fit onto the damaged bone in the ball and socket joint. Thanks to increasing medical advances, the quality of life of many people has improved with an artificial hip.

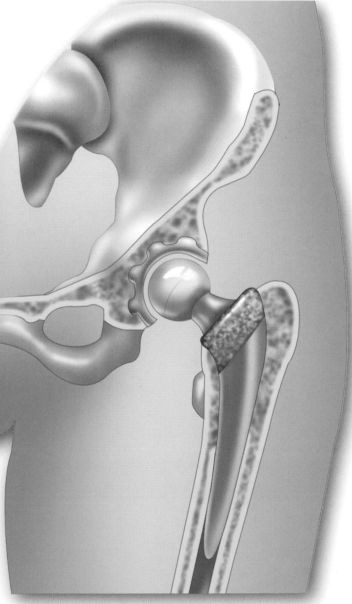

▲ Hip replacements are made from metal, ceramic or plastic.

A PROBLEM WITH BONES

Osteoporosis is the most common disease of the bones. Osteoporosis is a loss of bone tissue which weakens the bones, making them more likely to fracture and crumble. This reduces the strength and protection that bones give our body tissues. Osteoporosis occurs naturally in the elderly when bone tissue is made at a slower rate. Osteoporosis can also be accelerated in some women by the onset of the **menopause**. Many people do not know that they have the disease until they fracture a bone; usually the hip bone, which is under the most pressure. The following guidelines can help to prevent the onset of osteoporosis:

▶ **Eat a diet rich in calcium** – bone tissue is manufactured from calcium. Foods such as dairy products, beans and fish are sources of calcium.

▶ **Carry out weight-bearing exercise**, such as walking, jogging, aerobics and weight training – this strengthens your bones earlier in life so they can endure more as you get older.

▶ **Do not smoke and limit your intake of alcohol** – the effects of smoking and alcohol increase the chance of osteoporosis in later life.

▶ **Hormone replacement therapy** – some older women, who have passed through the menopause, are advised to take hormone replacement therapy to keep their bones strong.

TIME TRAVEL: DISCOVERIES OF THE PAST

▶ Ancient Egyptians are thought to have given us the first replacement body parts (prosthetics). Archaeologists have recently found a mummy of a women in her fifties that has a prosthetic toe. Her original toe had probably been amputated and the prosthetic toe was carved from wood and attached by leather strings.

Glossary

ANOREXIA NERVOSA – An eating disorder whereby a person starves themselves or tries to lose weight by other means so that they become dangerously thin. Anorexia nervosa is largely a psychological condition.

ANTIBODIES – Proteins in the blood that are produced by the immune system to destroy or weaken dangerous substances that could harm the body.

BASAL METABOLIC RATE – The rate at which energy is used by an organism at rest.

BLOOD PRESSURE – The pressure exerted by the blood against the walls of the blood vessels, particularly the arteries. Blood pressure varies with the strength of the heartbeat, the volume and thickness of the blood, the elasticity of the blood vessels and a person's age and general health.

BONE MARROW – The fatty tissue that fills some bones. Bone marrow is the main source of red blood cells, platelets and most white blood cells. Bone marrow releases up to 15 million new red blood cells every second.

BULIMIA – An eating disorder whereby a person binges and then tries to prevent weight gain (for example, by dieting or vomiting) so that they become dangerously thin. Like anorexia nervosa, bulimia is largely a psychological condition.

CALORIE – A unit of energy-producing potential that a source of food contains. A calorie is equal to the amount of energy required to raise the temperature of one gram of water by 1°C.

CARDIOLOGIST – A doctor who studies the structure and function of the heart and the circulatory system.

CARTILAGE – A tough, elastic tissue found in areas of the body, such as the joints, the nose and the ear. Cartilage helps to hold some of your bones together.

CELL – The smallest unit of an organism that is capable of functioning on its own. The human body contains over 200 cell types.

CHOLESTEROL – A fatty substance found in animal tissue and various foods. Cholesterol is an important feature of cell membranes but too much cholesterol in the blood can lead to heart disease and other circulatory conditions.

DEHYDRATION – An excessive loss of water from the body. Dehydration can be caused by an illness or by a lack of fluids. When a person becomes dehydrated, important salts are also lost from the body.

DENATURED – When a substance changes irreversibly. An egg is denatured when it is cooked.

ANSWERS

p11 Test yourself
Example answers: Carbohydrates – the primary source of energy for all body functions; eating too many carbohydrates can lead to weight gain; eating too few carbohydrates can lead to low energy levels. Proteins – help to maintain and replace the tissues in the body; eating too many proteins can lead to weight gain; eating too few proteins can limit healthy growth and development. Fats – the body's major energy storage system and also used to protect organs and bones, to

make hormones and to regulate blood pressure; eating too many fats can lead to weight gain and health problems such as heart disease, obesity and diabetes; eating too few fats can lead to weight loss, muscle loss and low energy levels. Vitamins and minerals – important substances that help the body to work effectively and to grow and develop; eating too many vitamins and minerals can cause an imbalance of chemicals in the body; eating too few vitamins and minerals can lead to a range of deficiency diseases.

p26 Test yourself
(1) Bladder
(2) Kidneys
(3) Renal artery
(4) Urethra

p30 Test yourself
Order of statements – 2, 5, 1, 3, 6, 4.
Ventricles have to pump blood all the way around the body.

DEOXYGENATED – To have dissolved oxygen removed (from the blood, for example).

DIFFUSION – The spontaneous movement of substances from an area of low concentration to an area of high concentration (or vice versa).

EMBRYO – An organism in its early stages of development.

ENZYMES – Proteins produced by living organisms that help to speed up chemical reactions.

GENETICS – The scientific study of heredity.

HORMONES – Chemical messengers produced by glands in the body. Hormones are transported by the blood to other organs to stimulate their function.

IMMUNE SYSTEM – A system of organs, tissues, cells and substances that protect the body against disease and infection.

LAXATIVE – A food or drug that stimulates the action of the intestines to remove waste from the body.

LIGAMENT – A tough, fibrous tissue that fastens bones or cartilage together at a joint.

LYMPHATIC SYSTEM – A network of vessels, carrying lymph, a tissue-cleansing fluid, from the tissues into the veins of the circulatory system.

MALNUTRITION – Poor nutrition which may be caused by a limited diet or by an illness.

MENOPAUSE – A natural occurrence in older women, when the menstrual cycle permanently stops.

NUTRIENT – Any substance that is nourishing or provides food for a living organism.

OBESITY – Increased body weight caused by an excessive accumulation of fat.

OXYGENATED – To be combined with oxygen.

PERISTALSIS – The wave-like muscle contractions that move food through the digestive system.

RESPIRATION – The process of releasing energy from food.

TENDON – The long, stringy cords that attach muscles to bones.

TOXIN – A poisonous substance produced by living cells, which can cause harm to the body.

Useful websites:
www.bbc.co.uk/schools
www.nationalgeographic.com
www.sciencenewsforkids.org
www.newscientist.com
www.howstuffworks.com

p33 Test yourself
Red blood cells – carry oxygen, sugars, vitamins and nutrients to cells around the body.
White blood cells – help to fight infection and are an important part of the immune system. There are two main types of white blood cells: phagocytes engulf foreign bodies that appear in the blood and lymphocytes produce antibodies.
Platelets – help the blood to clot so that a wound heals when you cut yourself.

p40 Test yourself
Example answers: Hinge joints – fingers, knees, elbows. Hinge joints allow movement in one direction only. Ball and socket joints – hips, shoulders. Ball and socket joints allow movement in all directions. Pivot joints – neck, the joint between the radius and ulna in the forearm. Pivot joints allow a rotating movement. Fixed joints – skull, pelvis. Fixed joints allow no movement. Gliding joints – vertebrae, fingers, toes. Gliding joints allow a limited amount of movement.

p43 Test yourself
On the blocks: thigh contracted (shortened) and hamstring, calf and shin muscles relaxed.
On the off: thigh muscle contracts to straighten the knee as it leaves the block, calf muscle contracts to straighten the ankle.

(1) A hair growing (smooth muscles)
(2) Swallowing (smooth muscles)
(3) Walking (skeletal muscles)

Index

Photo Credits – *(abbv: r, right, l, left, t, top, m, middle, b, bottom)* **Front cover images** Fotolia **p.1** (tr) Steve Gschmeissner/Science Photo Library (bl) www.istockphoto.com/Jeannette Meler Kamer (br) Denis Scott/Corbis **p.2** Corbis **p.3** (t) www.istockphoto.com/Jane Norton (b) www.istockphoto.com/Kelly Cline **p.4** (tl) www.istockphoto.com/Graça Victoria (tr) www.istockphoto.com/René Mansi (br) Clouds Hill Imaging Ltd/Corbis **p.5** Mark Clarke/Science Photo Library **p.6** (r) Corbis (l) Denis Scott/Corbis **p.7** www.istockphoto.com/Graça Victoria **p.8** (t) Craig Lovell/Corbis (b)www.istockphoto.com/Kelly Cline **p.9** www.istockphoto.com/René Mansi **p.10** (t) Corbis (b) www.istockphoto.com/Edyta Pawlowska **p.11** Jeffrey L. Rotman/Corbis **p.12** www.istockphoto.com **p.13** (tr) www.istockphoto.com/Sean Locke (bl) Vanessa Vick/Science Photo Library **p.14** www.istockphoto.com/Krzysztof Chrystowski **p.16** Gary Lee/uppa.co.uk **p.17** Lilly Lane/Corbis **p.18** Mark Clarke/Science Photo Library **p.20** J. C. Revy/Science Photo Library **p.21** (b) Digital Stock **p.22** (l) Chris Priest/Science Photo Library (r) Tracy Dominey/Science Photo Library **p.23** Leng/Leng/Corbis **p.24** (l) Susumu Nishinaga/Science Photo Library **p.26** Corbis **p.27** AJ Photo/Hop Americain/Science Photo Library **p.28** Bachrach's Studio, Boston **p.30** Bob Daemmrich/The Image Works **p.32** Clouds Hill Imaging Ltd/Corbis **p.33** (l) Steve Gschmeissner/Science Photo Library (r) Biology Media/Science Photo Library **p.34** (l) Sheila Terry/Science Photo Library **p.35** (t) Michael Nicholson/Corbis (b) Bettmann/Corbis **p.36** www.istockphoto.com/Shirley Bittner **p.37** (l) BSIP VEM/Science Photo Library (r) www.istockphoto.com/Jeannette Meler Kamer **p.38** (t) Carlos Dominquez/Corbis (b) John Fortunato Photography/Corbis **p.42** (m&r) Shutterstock/Q2A Creative **p.43** (t) Corbis (b) www.istockphoto.com/Jane Norton **p.44** (l) Philippe Plailly/Science Photo Library (m) Pasieka/Science Photo Library (r) Zephyr/Science Photo Library.